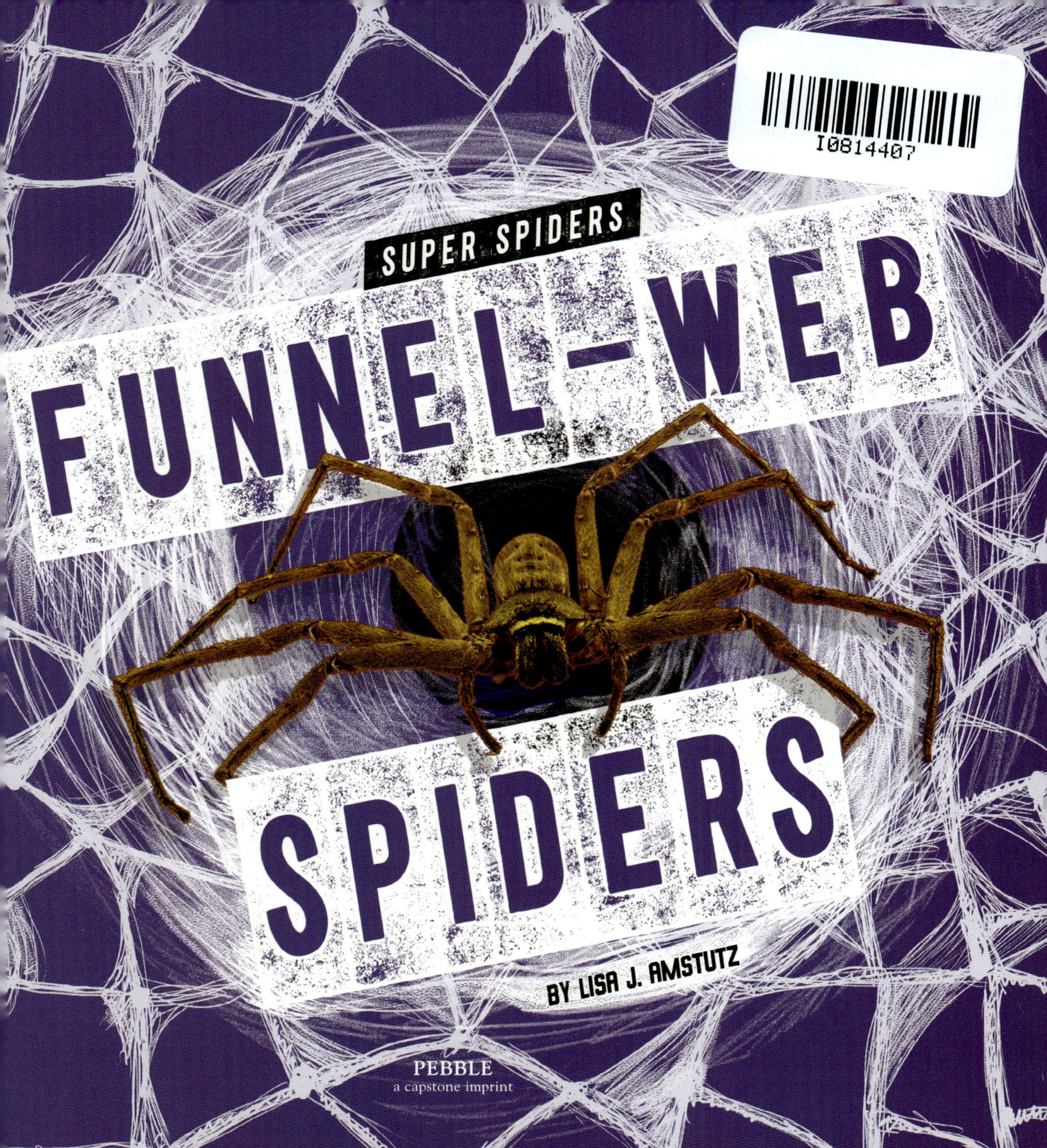
I0814407
SUPER SPIDERS
FUNNEL-WEB SPIDERS
BY LISA J. AMSTUTZ
PEBBLE
a capstone imprint

Published by Pebble, an imprint of Capstone
1710 Roe Crest Drive, North Mankato, Minnesota 56003
www.capstonepub.com

Library of Congress Cataloging-in-Publication Data is available on the Library of Congress website.
ISBN: 9798875224768 (hardcover)
ISBN: 9798875224515 (paperback)
ISBN: 9798875224720 (ebook PDF)

Summary: An introduction to funnel-web spiders, including how venomous they are, where they live, how they hunt, and more.

Editorial Credits
Editor: Ashley Kuehl; Designer: Kay Fraser; Media Researcher: Svetlana Zhurkin; Production Specialist: Whitney Schaefer

Image Credits
Capstone: Kay Fraser (spiderweb), cover and throughout; Getty Images: Bjoern Bartsch, 10, Ed Reschke, 11, Fug4s, 4, Ken Griffiths, 7, Mark_Breck, 5, scubaluna, 15, ShaftInAction, 19; Shutterstock: All Write studio (spiderweb), 4, 12, 16, Edwin Butter, 16, Evgenyrychko, 14, iceink (spider), cover, back cover, 1, Kamila Sankiewicz Photo, 18, Macronatura, 8, MarcinWojc, 17, Marek Mierzejewski, 12, Recep_Ozturk, 13, samray, 9, Sanjay M Dalvi, 6; Svetlana Zhurkin: 20

Printed and bound in China. 6274

TABLE OF CONTENTS

Words in **bold** are in the glossary.

MEET THE FUNNEL-WEB SPIDER

Look! A spider is spinning a web. Back and forth the spider moves. The web is shaped like a **funnel**. It leads into a small **burrow**. The spider crawls into the hole. It sits down to wait for a bug.

This spider is named for the shape of its web. Can you guess its name? It is called a funnel-web spider.

Funnel-web spiders live around the world. Most live in Australia. There are about 40 different kinds of funnel-web spiders. The Sydney funnel-web spider is the world's deadliest spider.

Don’t touch this spider! It has strong **fangs**. They can cut through a shoe or fingernail. The spider’s **venom** can kill a human. If one bites you, go to the doctor. They will give you medicine. It is called **antivenom**.

A funnel-web spider is big! It can be up to 3.1 inches (8 centimeters) long. It has a thick, shiny body. It can be black or brown. Like all spiders, it has two body parts. It has eight hairy legs.

The spider has **organs** that make **silk**. They are on its back end. A silk thread comes out. The spider forms it into a web.

Danger! A **predator** is near. Birds, lizards, and other animals eat spiders. The spider hides in its hole. It is safer there.

Funnel-web spiders live in cool, damp places. Some live under rocks and logs. Some live in grass.

THE CYCLE OF LIFE

In summer or fall, a male funnel-web spider leaves home. He wanders until he finds a female. He strokes her web. Will she let him into her home?

Yes! The pair mate. Then the female lays 100 to 200 eggs. They are in a silk sac. She keeps it safe from predators.

In a month, tiny spiders hatch. They stay with their mother for a few months. They shed their skin as they grow. This is called **molting**.

Then it is time to move out. The young spiders crawl away. They will make their own homes.

ON THE HUNT

A spider waits in its hole. Wiggle, wiggle! A bug steps on the web. The web is not sticky. But it is hard to walk on. The spider feels the web move. It darts out. Its strong legs grab its **prey**.

The spider mostly eats bugs. But it can eat other small animals too. A tiny lizard or snail makes a good meal.

Bite! The spider sinks in its fangs. The bug dies at once. Its insides turn to liquid. The spider can suck them out. It pulls the bug into its burrow to eat.

The spider is full. It will wait for its next meal to stop by!

MAKE A SPIDER

What You Need:

- pipe cleaners—white and black or brown

What You Do:

1. Twist eight white pipe cleaners together to make a funnel-shaped frame. Starting at the bottom, weave pipe cleaners in a spiral around the frame.
2. Cut two black or brown pipe cleaners in half. Twist them together in the middle.
3. Wind another pipe cleaner around the middle to make a spider's body. Bend spider's legs.
4. Set your spider at the bottom of the web.

SPIDER JOKES

What is a spider's favorite hobby?

Fly fishing!

What do you get when you cross a spider with a snowman?

frostbite

What did the spider do when he got a new computer?

He created a new web page.

What do spiders do for fun?

Surf the web!

GLOSSARY

antivenom (an-tee-VEN-uhm)—a medicine that helps the body fight off the effects of venom

burrow (BUHR-oh)—a hole in the ground made or used by an animal

fang (FANG)—the biting part of a spider's mouth

funnel (FUHN-uhl)—a cone shape with an open top and bottom

molting (MOHL-ting)—shedding an outer layer of skin

organ (OR-guhn)—a body part that has a special job

predator (PRED-uh-tur)—an animal that hunts other animals for food

prey (PRAY)—an animal hunted by another for food

silk (SILK)—long, thin threads

venom (VEN-uhm)—a poisonous liquid produced by some animals

READ MORE

Owen, Ruth. *Spiders: We're Not Scary—We're Amazing!* Minneapolis: Ruby Tuesday Books, 2024.

Pettiford, Rebecca. *Spiders*. Minneapolis: Bellwether Media, 2025.

Rose, Rachel. *Funnel-Web Spider*. Minneapolis: Bearport Publishing Company, 2024.

INTERNET SITES

ActiveWild: Sydney Funnel-Web Spider Facts, Picture, Video & Information
activewild.com/sydney-funnel-web-spider/

Britannica Kids: Spider
kids.britannica.com/kids/article/spider/353800

San Diego Zoo Wildlife Explorers: Spider
sdzwildlifeexplorers.org/animals/spider?keys=spider

INDEX

ABOUT THE AUTHOR

Lisa Amstutz is the author of more than 150 children's books on topics ranging from applesauce to zebra mussels. An ecologist by training, she enjoys sharing her love of nature with kids. Lisa lives on a small farm with her family.